Made in United States
North Haven, CT
01 December 2021

11780309R00074